# COLLEGE BASKETBALL
## UNDERDOG STORIES

BY HEATHER RULE

UNDERDOG SPORTS STORIES

SportsZone

An Imprint of Abdo Publishing | abdobooks.com

**abdobooks.com**

Published by Abdo Publishing, a division of ABDO, PO Box 398166, Minneapolis, Minnesota 55439.


Printed in the United States of America, North Mankato, Minnesota
092018
012019

THIS BOOK CONTAINS RECYCLED MATERIALS

Cover Photo: LM Otero/AP Images
Interior Photos: Rich Clarkson/NCAA Photos/Getty Images, 5; AP Images, 6, 8, 14, 17, 19, 22; Rich Clarkson/Sports Illustrated/Getty Images, 11; Jack Smith/AP Images, 13; Bill Kostroun/AP Images, 21; Bob Jordan/AP Images, 25; Gary Landers/AP Images, 26; Charles Rex Arbogast/AP Images, 29; Greg Nelson/Sports Illustrated/Getty Images, 31, 45; Tony Gutierrez/AP Images, 32, 35, 41; Eric Gay/AP Images, 37; David E. Klutho/Sports Illustrated/Getty Images, 38–39; Brynn Anderson/AP Images, 43

Editor: Patrick Donnelly
Series Designer: Melissa Martin

**Library of Congress Control Number: 2018949190**

**Publisher's Cataloging-in-Publication Data**

Names: Rule, Heather, author.
Title: College basketball underdog stories / by Heather Rule.
Description: Minneapolis, Minnesota : Abdo Publishing, 2019 | Series: Underdog sports stories | Includes online resources and index.
Identifiers: ISBN 9781532117602 (lib. bdg.) | ISBN 9781532170461 (ebook)
Subjects: LCSH: Basketball--Juvenile literature. | College athletes--Juvenile literature. | Upsets in sports--Juvenile literature. | Winning and losing--Juvenile literature.
Classification: DDC 796.323630--dc23

# TABLE OF CONTENTS

CHAPTER 1

# GAME CHANGER

One of the reasons we love sports is that they're unpredictable. Nobody knows what's going to happen in games, even if they give their best guess. Some of the most interesting sports stories in history happen when teams that aren't expected to win come out on top.

One of those moments came in 1966. The championship game of the National Collegiate Athletic Association (NCAA) men's basketball tournament has

Texas Western guard Bobby Joe Hill drives to the hoop against Kentucky.

TEXAS
14
KENT
3

provided many thrills over the years. But the final game of the 1966 tourney meant so much more than that. A quick glance around Maryland's Cole Field House that March evening showed that fans were witnessing history.

Kentucky's Thad Jaracz (55) and Texas Western's David Lattin fight for a rebound.

First, five players in the traditional blue-and-white uniforms of the University of Kentucky strolled onto the court to represent the top-ranked Wildcats in the starting lineup. Then the Texas Western Miners, dressed in orange, joined their opponents at center court.

If the Texas Western players had looked at the crowd, they might have seen fans waving a Confederate flag. It also would have been hard to miss another fact: the opponents, game officials, cheerleaders, and sportswriters were all white.

When the Texas Western players stepped onto the court that night, they made college basketball history. They were the first team to field an all-black starting lineup in a NCAA championship game. Miners coach Don Haskins only used two reserves in the title game. They were both black, too. Meanwhile, four white players and one Hispanic player remained on the bench. For Haskins, it wasn't about race. He just used the best players he had.

Miners coach Don Haskins, *center*, is congratulated while his players celebrate after upsetting Kentucky.

The game itself wasn't filled with special drama or last-second shots. The Miners grabbed an early lead with a free throw from Nevil Shed to make it 10–9 and didn't look back from there. They won the game 72–65 for their first national championship. Texas Western held Kentucky to a 38.6 shooting percentage, a season-low for the Wildcats. The game won't be recognized for star-filled lineups or dazzling performances. It will be remembered because of the lasting effect it had on basketball in the years to come.

The game was held during the peak of the civil rights movement. This championship game pitting an all-white team against an all-black team brought racial issues to light in a sporting venue. At the time, many white fans and media didn't think black players were mentally tough or disciplined enough to be consistent winners. Sure, they said, black players were very athletic, but in the end, they wouldn't be able to play cohesive team basketball, especially against white athletes. But the Miners showed the flaw in this line of thinking with their consistent and methodical play in their championship victory over Kentucky.

Future Hall of Famer Pat Riley was a forward on that Kentucky team. Riley went on to win five professional championships as the coach of the Los Angeles Lakers and the Miami Heat. He once called the 1966 title game "the Emancipation Proclamation of college basketball" because of the role it played in ending the segregation of athletics.

## RUPP DRAGS HIS HEELS

University of Kentucky president John W. Oswald saw change was on the horizon in the Civil Rights era. He tried to convince coach Adolph Rupp to recruit a black player. Rupp held out, even after other SEC schools such as Auburn and Mississippi had integrated their teams. The Wildcats finally dressed a black player in December 1970. Rupp retired at the end of the next season.

The Southeastern Conference (SEC)—of which Kentucky was a charter member—was still segregated in 1966, two years after

Kentucky coach Adolph Rupp, *right*, and his players look dejected after losing to Texas Western in the 1966 NCAA title game.

the Civil Rights Act had passed. In the 1966–67 season, Vanderbilt's Perry Wallace was the SEC's first black athlete to play on a scholarship.

Decades later, it's barely noteworthy to see racial diversity on the basketball court. The Texas Western Miners can take credit for this with their 1966 underdog champions.

CHAPTER 2

# THE CARDIAC KIDS

In 1982–83 North Carolina State had a decent men's basketball team—decent, but not great. The Wolfpack lost 10 games in the regular season and almost didn't make the NCAA tournament. No team had ever won a national championship with 10 losses beside its name.

But led by their head coach, an excitable young New Yorker named Jim Valvano, the Wolfpack got hot at the right time. They entered the Atlantic Coast Conference (ACC) postseason tournament unranked and seeded

North Carolina State coach Jim Valvano works the sideline during an NCAA Tournament game in 1983.

fourth of eight teams. They squeaked out a one-point win over Wake Forest in the opening round. In the semifinals, they took Michael Jordan and fifth-ranked North Carolina to overtime before pulling away 91–84. Finally, in the ACC

North Carolina State guard Dereck Whittenburg gets off a shot in traffic against Virginia during the 1983 NCAA Tournament.

championship game, they shocked All-American center Ralph Sampson and Virginia—the No. 2 team in the nation—with an 81–78 victory.

That run clinched a berth in the NCAA tournament for North Carolina State. But as the sixth seed in the West Region, the Wolfpack weren't expected to advance very far. In fact, they almost bowed out in their first game. They trailed 11th-seeded Pepperdine by six points with just 24 seconds left in overtime, but they rallied for a 69–67 victory in double overtime.

But Valvano's team was just getting started. From there, the Wolfpack upset the third seed (and No. 6 team in the nation), the University of Nevada-Las Vegas (UNLV), 71–70 to reach the Sweet 16. They also got a little help from Utah, which had upset the seventh-ranked University of California, Los Angeles (UCLA) in the same round. The Wolfpack cruised past the Utes by 19, setting up a rematch with Virginia.

North Carolina State had lost to Virginia twice in the regular season. But the Wolfpack followed their ACC tournament win with another victory over Sampson's Cavaliers, this time 63–62. Against all odds, the Wolfpack were heading to the Final Four.

North Carolina State met No. 18 Georgia in the first semifinal, but that was just an appetizer for what was to come. The other semifinal pitted No. 1 Houston against No. 2 Louisville. Most observers figured the winner of that game would take home the title, especially after the unranked Wolfpack beat Georgia 67–60 to advance to the title game. Houston and Louisville traded big jump shots and thunderous dunks all night, and the Cougars overcame a five-point halftime deficit to win 94–81.

One game remained to determine the national championship. Houston's roster was stacked with elite talent, including future Hall of Famers Akeem "the Dream" Olajuwon and Clyde "the Glide" Drexler. Nobody on the

Wolfpack had a nickname that cool. However, people began calling the team "the Cardiac Kids" for all of their last-second heroics. The Wolfpack had one more heart-stopper in store for their fans.

The score was tied 52–52 in the final 30 seconds. North Carolina State worked the ball around the court,

Led by center Akeem Olajuwon, Houston liked to play above the rim.

## MAKING A DIFFERENCE

A decade after North Carolina State won the national championship, Valvano died of cancer at age 47. Before he died, "Jimmy V" and ESPN established the V Foundation for Cancer Research. One hundred percent of its proceeds benefit cancer research.

trying to find an open shot. Guard Dereck Whittenburg barely controlled a pass 30 feet away from the basket. With time running out, Whittenburg heaved a desperation shot that came up short. But teammate Lorenzo Charles jumped up near the hoop, grabbed the ball out of the air, and slammed it through the hoop for the game-winning basket.

Charles connected for the dunk with one second left, and the clock ran out as the Wolfpack began to celebrate. Valvano ran around the court in the pandemonium. Fans and players mobbed the court.

Lorenzo Charles slams home the game-winning basket against Houston.

"The Cardiac Kids have done it!" CBS announcer Brent Musburger exclaimed. The Wolfpack had written the ultimate Cinderella story, one that underdogs will be compared to for years to come.

CHAPTER 3

# DETHRONING A DYNASTY

In the 1984–85 season, no team was more feared than Georgetown. The Hoyas ruled college basketball with strength and style. The defending national champions were led by senior center Patrick Ewing, a three-time first-team All-America selection. An intimidating shot blocker and rebounder, Ewing won the Naismith Award as the country's best player that season. Meanwhile, junior David Wingate and sophomore Reggie Williams were

Patrick Ewing was a feared shot blocker and dominant rebounder for Georgetown.

GEORGETOWN
WILLIAMS
34
30
23

silky-smooth perimeter players who shared the scoring duties with Ewing.

The Hoyas were ranked No. 1 in the nation in the first and last polls of the regular season. They entered the

Villanova's Ed Pinckney grabs a rebound in the Wildcats' upset of Maryland in the Sweet 16.

NCAA tournament 30–2 and were the decided favorite to add a second straight title to their résumé. Then they rolled through their first five games to reach the championship game at Kentucky's Rupp Arena.

Georgetown's opponent was a familiar one. The Villanova Wildcats were fellow members of the Big East Conference. The Hoyas had already beaten Villanova twice that season—a two-point overtime win in Philadelphia and a 57–50 victory back at home in Washington, DC. The third time, however, would be a different story.

It had been an up-and-down year for the Wildcats, whose 18–9 regular-season record left them on the bubble of being selected for the NCAA tournament. They did well enough in the Big East tournament to qualify for "the big dance" as the No. 8 seed in the Southeast Region. But it almost came apart in the first round before the Wildcats eked out a 51–49 victory over Dayton on a late basket by guard Harold Jensen.

Then Villanova began a string of upsets with a 59–55 win over top-seeded Michigan. In the Sweet 16 the Wildcats defeated No. 5 seed Maryland by three. Then they overcame a five-point halftime deficit and blew out second-seeded North Carolina 56–44 to reach the Final Four in Lexington, Kentucky.

The run continued as the Wildcats got 19 points from Dwayne McClain and held All-American Keith Lee to just 10 in a 52–45 victory over Memphis, the second seed in the Midwest. That set up Villanova's third shot at Georgetown,

## ALMOST PERFECT

Wildcats players put up some crazy shooting numbers in the title game. Dwayne McClain and Ed Pinckney each were 5-for-7 from the field. They also combined to make 13 of 15 free throws. Harold Jensen made all five of his field goal attempts. Gary McLain was 3-for-3, and Harold Pressley finished 4-for-6. The five starters only sat for a total of nine minutes.

Ewing swats away a shot taken by Villanova's Harold Pressley.

which had throttled fellow No. 1 seed St. John's in the other semifinal.

As a No. 8 seed, Villanova was the lowest seed to reach the championship game. Then the Wildcats went out and proved they belonged. In the era before the shot clock (the NCAA would adopt it the next season), Villanova was able to slow down the pace of the game and keep Ewing, Wingate, and Williams in check.

Pinckney and his teammates rejoice after stunning Georgetown.

Still, the Wildcats would need to be incredibly efficient on offense if they were to pull off the upset. And that's exactly what happened. Villanova made 22 of its 28 shots (78.6 percent) from the field. The Wildcats took just 10 shots in the second half—and they made nine of them. Dwayne McClain scored a game-high 17. Ed Pinckney played while sick with the flu and still managed 16 points and six rebounds.

At the end of the game, all Villanova had to do was get the ball in bounds and hold on for two seconds to run out the clock. McClain stumbled to the hardwood floor and reached out to grab the ball. Georgetown's Wingate hovered over him in disbelief as McClain pulled the ball close to his chest and secured it with his arms. Then he pumped his left arm high in the air to celebrate one of the most shocking upsets in NCAA basketball history. Villanova had dethroned the champs in the first year the NCAA tournament housed a full 64-team bracket.

CHAPTER 4

# FIRST FOUR TO FINAL FOUR

Virginia Commonwealth University (VCU) lost four of its last five games at the end of the 2010–11 regular season. The Rams rallied to win two games in the Colonial Athletic Association conference tournament but lost to Old Dominion in the title game. That was barely enough to get the Rams into the NCAA tournament. But they sure made the most of their appearance.

The 2011 tournament was the first to include 68 teams. Four games that were essentially play-in contests whittled

VCU forward Jamie Skeen (21) outmuscles two Purdue players to get off a shot during the NCAA tournament.

PURDUE
25
VCU
21
VCU
12

the field to its standard 64. VCU was matched up against Southern California in one of those games. The Rams won 59–46 to earn the 11th seed in the Southwest Region.

Then VCU really got on a roll. It beat sixth-seeded Georgetown by 18 points. Then the Rams crushed No. 13 Purdue, the region's third seed, 94–76 to reach the Sweet 16.

That game, against fellow Cinderella Florida State, the region's No. 10 seed, went to overtime tied 65–65. VCU was down a point with seven seconds to play in overtime, in need of a bucket to extend the tournament run. Bradford Burgess took an inbound pass and hit a driving layup for the win. VCU coach Shaka Smart bounced around the court pumping his fists as his team reached the regional final.

Surely this would be the end of the line. VCU faced top-seeded Kansas, the No. 2 team in the nation. But it was barely even a ballgame. The Rams—who were

11-point underdogs that day—surged out to a 14-point halftime lead and held on for a 71–61 shocker. VCU's strong defensive effort limited the Jayhawks to just 35.5 percent shooting from the field. Meanwhile, the Rams

Brandon Burgess, *left*, hits the winning shot to beat Florida State.

Shaka Smart (blue shirt) and his assistant coaches call a play against Kansas.

hit a season-high 12 three-point attempts, shooting a blistering 48 percent from beyond the arc.

Only two other No. 11-seed teams before them ever made it to the Final Four. One reporter even speculated that VCU making the Final Four was the most unlikely scenario to occur in the NCAA tournament in the past 25 years.

VCU was the first team in tournament history to start in the First Four and reach the Final Four. The Rams also won an ESPY award for Best Upset with the victory over Kansas to reach the Final Four.

## KID COACH

VCU coach Shaka Smart was just 33 years old and in his second season as a head coach when he guided the Rams to the Final Four. It was the school's 10th NCAA tournament appearance, and it started a streak of seven straight seasons in the big dance for the Rams. The Rams were 5–9 all time in the tourney before Smart arrived. He led them to a 7–5 tournament mark in five seasons.

VCU's run finally ended when it ran into another small-conference school accustomed to overachieving. Eighth-seeded Butler came through the Southeast Region, defeating the Nos. 1, 2, and 4 seeds along the way. The Bulldogs then knocked off VCU 70–62 in the national semifinals.

CHAPTER 5

# BULLDOGS BITE BACK

The women's basketball team at the University of Connecticut (UConn) is one of the mightiest dynasties in all sports. Under head coach Geno Auriemma, the Huskies won 11 national championships between 1995 and 2016. They've also put together three of the longest winning streaks in college basketball history. Every time UConn loses, it makes headlines. But one of those defeats was more epic than the rest.

Connecticut's Napheesa Collier (24) and Mississippi State's Chinwe Okorie battle for a rebound.

UCONN
24
#WFinalFour

## CRIMSON SURPRISE

Harvard All-American Allison Feaster scored 35 points and grabbed 13 rebounds in the first round of the 1998 NCAA tournament. That monster game helped her team become the first No. 16 seed to defeat a No. 1 seed in any NCAA tournament, as the Crimson knocked off top-seeded Stanford 71–67 on its home court.

Few would have expected Mississippi State (MSU) to be the team that took down the Huskies. The teams had met in the 2016 NCAA tournament, and UConn hammered the Bulldogs 98–38 on the way to another national title. When they squared off the next year in the national semifinals, the Huskies were riding a 111-game winning streak. But the Bulldogs were ready for redemption.

MSU raced out to a 16-point lead in the second quarter. That was the largest deficit the Huskies faced during their historic streak. But UConn didn't give up.

The Huskies stormed back to tie the game 60–60 at the end of regulation.

The Bulldogs were clinging to a two-point lead in the final 30 seconds of overtime when MSU guard Dominique Dillingham was called for a controversial flagrant foul. Her arm made contact with the throat of UConn's Katie Lou Samuelson as the two were reaching for the ball. Samuelson calmly made both free throws to tie the game.

Morgan William (2) launches her last-second shot against UConn.

UConn still had the ball with 26.6 seconds to play. The Huskies could have held the ball and taken the last shot, but MSU's pressure defense forced UConn into a bad shot that fell short and rolled out of bounds.

The Bulldogs had the ball with 12.3 seconds to go. Dillingham dribbled the ball past midcourt as the clock ticked down. She passed it to Morgan William, MSU's lightning-quick point guard. William faked left, drove to the right, then popped up with the ball for an off-balance 15-foot jump shot. The ball sailed over the UConn defenders and swished through the hoop just as the clock ran out.

William turned and screamed toward the sky, overwhelmed by the excitement of

William came through in the clutch for the underdog Bulldogs.

the moment. Then her teammates stormed the floor in celebration and piled on top of her. The game was over, and so was UConn's record 111-game winning streak. Mississippi State had dethroned mighty UConn with a 66–64 overtime victory.

Auriemma was gracious in defeat, calmly gathering his disappointed players and giving the Bulldogs time to celebrate before the postgame handshakes. He also embraced William and MSU head coach Vic Schaefer, congratulating them on the remarkable victory.

Though the Bulldogs pulled off the ultimate upset in the semifinal, they lost 67–55 to South Carolina in the national title game. But they'll always be remembered as the team that took down a dynasty.

CHAPTER 6

# LOYOLA'S SECRET WEAPON

Going into the 2018 NCAA men's tournament, most people weren't expecting much from Loyola, a small Jesuit university in Chicago. The Ramblers had won the Missouri Valley Conference regular-season and tournament championships. But they entered the NCAA tournament as the No. 11 seed in the South Region. A quick exit was Loyola's most likely fate.

However, the Ramblers had a secret weapon. It wasn't a new lineup or a trick play or a unique strategy. It was a

Loyola's Donte Ingram celebrates his buzzer beater against Miami.

0.0
61
62

## A YEAR OF UPSETS

The ultimate upset of a No. 16 seed beating a No. 1 had not happened in the men's tournament since the field expanded to 64 teams in 1985. But in 2018, the University of Maryland-Baltimore County dominated Virginia 74–54 in the first round, and the men's tourney finally had its first 16-over-1 upset.

98-year-old nun who became one of the biggest stories of the entire tournament.

Sister Jean Dolores Schmidt, known as "Sister Jean," had been the team chaplain since 1994. She attended as many home games as possible, leading the team in pregame prayers. She liked to wear maroon sneakers with "Sister" and "Jean" stitched in gold on the left and right heels of the shoes.

And she knew her hoops, too. When head coach Porter Moser was hired in 2011, Sister Jean left a folder on his desk complete with notes and scouting reports.

Even though the Ramblers were a No. 11 seed, Sister Jean picked them to reach the Sweet 16 in her personal bracket. The team fulfilled her prediction—and then some.

Sister Jean was the talk of the tournament during Loyola's run to the Final Four.

In the opening round against sixth-seeded Miami, the Ramblers trailed by a point with 10 seconds to play. Then senior guard Donte Ingram drained a long three-pointer that just beat the buzzer, giving Loyola a 64–62 win.

The Ramblers were just getting started. In the second round they took down Tennessee, the region's No. 3 seed, 63–62. In the Sweet 16 they pulled out another one-point win, this time 69–68 over seventh-seeded Nevada. Loyola finally broke things open with a 78–62 victory over ninth-seeded Kansas State in the Elite Eight.

That last victory earned the Ramblers a significant spot in basketball history. They became the fourth No. 11 seed to ever make it to the Final Four. Loyola hadn't even been to the tournament in more than 30 years. The Ramblers did it with a balanced lineup. Five players averaged between 10.5 and 13.2 points per game. None of them were big names or five-star recruits out of high school.

Loyola coach Porter Moser consoles Marques Townes as time runs down against Michigan.

Also, they shot 50.7 percent from the floor as a team, the third best mark in the country.

Ultimately, Loyola's run ended in the national semifinal with a 69–57 loss to Michigan, the No. 7 team in the country. The Cinderella season was over, and so was a 14-game winning streak for the Ramblers, who hadn't lost a game since January.

# GLOSSARY

**Cinderella**

In sports, a player or team that achieves much greater success than expected.

**civil rights movement**

An organized drive during the 1950s and 1960s advocating for the legal rights of African American citizens.

**conference**

A group of schools that join together to create a league for their sports teams.

**perimeter**

The outside edge of an object; in basketball, it refers to a shot outside the free-throw lane.

**seed**

A ranking assigned to a team that determines its opponents in a tournament.

**shot clock**

A timer in basketball that indicates how much time a team has left before it has to take a shot at the basket.

**underdog**

The person or team that is not expected to win.

**upset**

An unexpected victory by a supposedly weaker team or player.

# MORE INFORMATION

## BOOKS


Maraniss, Andrew. *Strong Inside: The True Story of How Perry Wallace Broke College Basketball's Color Line*. New York: Philomel Books, 2017.

Rappoport, Ken. *Biggest Upsets in Sports*. Minneapolis, MN: Abdo Publishing, 2014.

Wilner, Barry. *The Biggest Upsets of All Time*. Minneapolis, MN: Abdo Publishing, 2016.


# ONLINE RESOURCES

Booklinks
NONFICTION NETWORK
FREE! ONLINE NONFICTION RESOURCES

To learn more about college basketball underdogs, visit **abdobooklinks.com**. These links are routinely monitored and updated to provide the most current information available.

# INDEX



# ABOUT THE AUTHOR

Heather Rule is a writer, sports journalist, and social media coordinator. She has a bachelor's degree in journalism and mass communication from the University of St. Thomas.